Little Laureates

South London
Edited by Lynsey Hawkins

Young Writers

First published in Great Britain in 2007 by:
Young Writers
Remus House
Coltsfoot Drive
Peterborough
PE2 9JX
Telephone: 01733 890066
Website: www.youngwriters.co.uk

All Rights Reserved

© *Copyright Contributors 2007*

SB ISBN 978-1 84602 939 4

Foreword

Young Writers was established in 1991 and has been passionately devoted to the promotion of reading and writing in children and young adults ever since. The quest continues today. Young Writers remains as committed to the nurturing of poetic and literary talent as ever.

This year's Young Writers competition has proven as vibrant and dynamic as ever and we are delighted to present a showcase of the best poetry from across the UK and in some cases overseas. Each poem has been selected from a wealth of *Little Laureates* entries before ultimately being published in this, our sixteenth primary school poetry series.

Once again, we have been supremely impressed by the overall quality of the entries we have received. The imagination, energy and creativity which has gone into each young writer's entry made choosing the poems a challenging and often difficult but ultimately hugely rewarding task - the general high standard of the work submitted ensured this opportunity to bring their poetry to a larger appreciative audience.

We sincerely hope you are pleased with this final collection and that you will enjoy *Little Laureates South London* for many years to come.

Contents

Alderbrook Primary School
Danny Khan (9)	1
Muminah Rasul (8)	2
Eliyaz Saraj (8)	3

Archbishop Sumner CE Primary School
Anthony Iyawe (7)	4
Nana Nkyidjour (8)	5
Scott Dyke (8)	6
Udoka Adibe (7)	7
Jayden Taylor (8)	8
Tamara Manley (9)	9
Adijat Giwa (10)	10
Sophie Douglas (9)	11
Bola Olanrewaju (9)	12
Anita Iyawe (11)	13
Tafote A Akerejola (10)	14
Joshua Xtian (10)	15
Nicole Boahene-Asomah (11)	16
Melisa Armental (10)	17
Jenise Henry-Mclean (11)	18
Aishat Adetunji (10)	19
Reece Wallace (11)	20
Olayimika Olayanju-Olagbegi (10)	21
Jordan Patrick-Asuman (11)	22
Morayo Fadiya (8)	23
Ayeshia Adenugba (9)	24
Yohanna Ephrem (8)	25
Daisy Chamberlain (8)	26
Ryan Lawal (8)	27
Matthew Lewis (8)	28
Lauren Moseley (8)	29
Siana Douglas Keise (11)	30
Isaac Danso (11)	31
Gabrielle Danso (8)	32
Abigail Sarpong (8)	33

Our Lady of Victories Primary School
Madeleine Oliver (9)	34

Clemmie Pollard (9)	36
Harry Bound (9)	38
William Eacott (9)	39
Lauren Wright (8)	40
Conor Larkin (8)	41
Anthony Corless (8)	42
Emily McMahon (8)	43
Jack Smith (8)	44
Andrew Porter (8)	45
Jessica Taylor (8)	46
Lucas Tishler (8)	48
Declan Thompson (8)	49

St John's CE Primary School, Penge

Daniel Bonner Hillier (10)	50
Amy Louise Brenson (9)	51
Amy McLauchlan (9)	52
Rebecca Blizzard (9)	53
Max Billy Edwards-May (10)	54
Taja Hippolyte-Wells (9)	55
Jadzia Samuel (9)	56
Elliott Dyer (10)	57
Sadie Angela Jordan (9)	58
Siobhan McShane (9)	59
Tia Jane Angel (10)	60
Matthew Steenson (8)	61
Kyle Manning (9)	62
Emma Prempeh (10)	63

Stockwell Primary School

Micheal Iluyomade (7)	64
Zeinab Troare (8)	65
Leila Bewshear (7)	66
Scott Greenfield (8)	67
Abdulhafiz Malak (7)	68
Aisha Lutumba (10)	69
Salomé Ferreira Castro Silva (10)	70
Royan Moore (11)	71
Benedicte Makamu (9)	72
Tesfa Atere (9)	73
Aminah Turay (10)	74

Nana Akua-Afriyie (11)	75
Tameka Salmon (11)	76
Ellis Thomas (11)	77
Chelsea Beckford Tunisa (11)	78
Honey Brion Thompson (10)	79
Djenne Payne-Pemberton (10)	80
Hassan Mugga (10)	81
Kevaun McKenzie (10)	82
Joâo Diogo Fernandes Conceicâo (10)	83
Ramone St Louis (11)	84
Ramon Oluseye (8)	85
Ishmael Lartey (8)	86
Tavio Wright (8)	87
Ryan Stoker (10)	88
Nicole Jessica Figueira de Sousa (7)	89
Anastasia Carvalho (7)	90
Ana Gomes (10)	91

Thorntree Primary School

Payge Gregory (9)	92
Luke Cheal (9)	93
Esther Agbara (9)	94
Tommy Amis (8)	95
George Ball (9)	96
Sade Sangar (7)	97
Danny Fryer (7)	98
Quinn Smith-Suckoo (7)	99
Darcy Clinton (7)	100
Katie Chapman (7)	101
Abbie Carter (8)	102
Ibukun Agbara (7)	103
Rebeccah Love (7)	104
Joseph Newman (7)	105
Salma Salah (7)	106
Matthew Coleman (8)	107
Sam Green (8)	108
George Power (7)	109
Harrison O'Donoghue (7)	110
Kristen Tedham (10)	111
Connor Gregory (10)	112
Glenn Nutton (10)	113

Georgie Devito (10)	114
Kiera Murphy (10)	115
Danielle White (10)	116
Ryan Carter (10)	117
Stephanie Rouse (10)	118
Asten Brown (10)	119
Storm Smith-Suckoo (10)	120
Marie-Jo Djedje (11)	121
Zoe Rennie (10)	122
Zoë Mansbridge (9)	123
Donique Shallow (9)	124
Zoë Mullord (9)	125
Kayley O'Donoghue (9)	126
Chloe Burton (9)	127
Lucy Newman (9)	128
Claire Slaughter (10)	129
Kayleigh Grant (10)	130
Brandon Bissenden (10)	131
Chinua Joseph-Collins (9)	132
Scott Richard (10)	133
Jack Lee Kiely (9)	134
Jamie Seymour (9)	135
Chukwuma Aliago (9)	136
Alex Coleman (10)	137
Charlie Barrett (9)	138
Oliver Marlow (8)	139
Leighvi Pilcher (9)	140
Carl White (9)	141
Christina Summerfield (10)	142
Daisy Golding (8)	143

The Poems

The Writer Of This Poem
(Based on 'The Writer of this Poem' by Roger McGough)

The writer of this poem
Is as slow as a turtle
As fast as a Ferrari
As super as Superman.

The writer of this poem
Is as spiky as a hedgehog
As big as an elephant
As tiny as an ant.

The writer of this poem
Is as funny as a comedian
As fantastic as a film star
As rubbish as trash.

The writer of this poem
Is taller than a tree
As keen as the north wind
As clever as a tick.

*'He's one in a million billion
(Or so the poem says).'*

Danny Khan (9)
Alderbrook Primary School

Haunted School

Look through the gate of the haunted school,
What can you see? What can you see?
The haunted school!
The haunted school!
Oh no there's monsters in the swimming pool.

Look through the classrooms of the haunted school,
What can you see? What can you see?
The haunted classrooms!
The haunted classrooms!
With five witches on the class brooms.

Look through the windows of the haunted office,
What can you see? What can you see?
The haunted office!
The haunted office!
Oh no it's the headless ghost of Professor Boris.

Look through the doors of the haunted hall,
What can you see? What can you see?
The haunted hall!
The haunted hall!
Oh no the monsters are playing with a head for a ball.

OK now I better run because the monsters have had enough
And are getting tough
And if I get caught I don't think I'll have fun.

Muminah Rasul (8)
Alderbrook Primary School

Happy Families

Happy families living as one,
Happy families eating dinner,
Happy families having fun,
Happy families are a winner.

Eliyaz Saraj (8)
Alderbrook Primary School

An Egyptian Farmer

Where golden sand meets water farmers fish,
Where River Nile flows we collect fresh water,
Where cows meet shining seeds they stamp,
Where crystal water meets sand they sail.

Anthony Iyawe (7)
Archbishop Sumner CE Primary School

Egyptian Farmer

When the hot sun meets the see-through river, we drink,
When golden sand meets feet, we stamp on the clean seeds,
When rough wooden boats meet busy rivers, we fish,
When golden wheat meets hand, we touch,
When tired people meet shade, we rest.

Nana Nkyidjour (8)
Archbishop Sumner CE Primary School

A Egyptian Farmer

Where the hard working meets golden sand, we make bread,
Where cow meets hard sand, we stamp,
Where man meets grain, we shake,
Where strong men meets soft sand, we dig,
Where cows meet Nile, we carry heavy water.

Scott Dyke (8)
Archbishop Sumner CE Primary School

An Egyptian Farmer

When young men meet soft cats, they care,
Where Egyptian people meet prickly sand, they dig,
Where the strong cows meet sand they stamp,
Where the Nile meets flashing sun, we work hard,
Where people see wonderful wheat, they cut,
Where the girls see the delicious fish, they eat.

Udoka Adibe (7)
Archbishop Sumner CE Primary School

Egyptian Farmer

When brutal cow meets golden sand, we stamp,
When wooden bowl meets crystal seeds, we shake,
When wooden boat meets crystal river, we sail,
When fishing net meets water, we fish,
When hard branch meets cosy leaf, we grow.

Jayden Taylor (8)
Archbishop Sumner CE Primary School

I Have A Dream . . .

I have a dream . . . I have a dream that
White people and black people can
Live in peace and harmony.
The world will be full of equality and love forever.

I have a dream that we should be like a family,
Like sisters and brothers and we could have a polite world.

I have a dream that we could be a whole community
And we could have friendship with us today.

I have a dream that goodwill spreads out through the world.

I have a dream that we should stop violence.

Tamara Manley (9)
Archbishop Sumner CE Primary School

I Have A Dream

I have a dream that we could live in harmony,
I have a dream that sympathy will surround us,
I have a dream that we could all hand in hand be one family,
I have a dream that white people and black people could be friends,
I have a dream that peace could be on our earth.

Adijat Giwa (10)
Archbishop Sumner CE Primary School

Dream

I have a dream . . .
I have a dream that one day,
We can see we need to live in
A world with peace and friendship,
I am going to promise you that
I will try and prevent violence,
I will try to make world peace
And if I don't succeed,
At least I can say,
I tried but still I will try
And make it my goal.

Sophie Douglas (9)
Archbishop Sumner CE Primary School

Dream

I have a dream,
I have a dream that peace should be everywhere,
I have a dream that sympathy should be in everybody.
I have a dream that harmony should be here now . . .
I have a dream that good will spread everywhere.

Bola Olanrewaju (9)
Archbishop Sumner CE Primary School

Love

Love is the sweet smell of perfume,
It is emotions,
Which come from your heart,
Love is passion -
Love is a mixture of passion and delight.

Love is a mixture of sweetness and joy,
Love the sound of peace,
Love is luxurious,
Love can never be touched by hate.

Love is like a flower,
Blooming in the spring,
Love feels like sitting on a cloud
And surrounded by rings.

Anita Iyawe (11)
Archbishop Sumner CE Primary School

Happiness

Happiness is a fabulous feeling
That pounds in your heart for joy.

Happiness attracts love,
It is a feeling that makes the world rejoice.

When happiness is nowhere to be found,
You feel so uncomfortable,
The colour of happiness is white,
Happiness is a feeling that makes you feel relieved,
Happiness sounds like being alive without having any problems,
Happiness is the opposite of sadness,
Happiness is love,
Happiness is incredible,
Happiness is better than money.

Tafote A Akerejola (10)
Archbishop Sumner CE Primary School

Fear

Fear smells like dark smoke,
Fear feels like a savage strangling you until you choke,
Fear tastes like a sour sweet stuck in your throat.

Don't think you can survive,
Fear is fear, and that's life!
Fear makes your heart pound,
Fear is an unpleasant sound.

Joshua Xtian (10)
Archbishop Sumner CE Primary School

Sadness

Tears welling up and all I feel is pain,
The bleakness I feel will never be happiness,
Maybe the joy has been sucked out of me,
Like a balloon losing air,
My emotions, my thoughts, the thing I love,
It doesn't matter anymore because a sadness spell is on me.

Sadness is not contagious,
It happens when people feel it,
Deep, deep inside themselves,
A sad, dismal feeling.

A tear drops to the ground,
One of the memories I lose,
Sadness is a horrible feeling,
The happy memories are a long, way away.

Nicole Boahene-Asomah (11)
Archbishop Sumner CE Primary School

Happiness

Happiness is a smile,
Everybody loves a smile,
Smiles make me smile.

Every time I look at people with a smile,
They look back at me with a sparkling smile,
I like the way they smile because it fills me up with joy.

Melisa Armental (10)
Archbishop Sumner CE Primary School

Fear

Fear is a feeling that everyone gets,
Fear is a feeling that gives you a threat,
The colour of fear is red, black and blue,
Sometimes it will sneak up on you.

It lurks in the dark when nobody's around,
It will surprise you when you're not aware,
It tastes foul,
It looks nightmarish.

Fear is everywhere -
It's where you step, it's where you sleep,
It sounds like a bat screeching in the wind,
That's what fear is all about.

Jenise Henry-Mclean (11)
Archbishop Sumner CE Primary School

Love

Love is something you'll never forget,
Or love is something you'll never regret,
Very soft and tender love,
Every person deserves true love.

Love is something you feel inside you,
Or love is something you know is true,
Very sweet and sour love,
Every person deserves true love.

Love can make you feel passion,
Or love can make you feel affection,
Very passionate and tender love,
Emotional love comes from above.

Aishat Adetunji (10)
Archbishop Sumner CE Primary School

Hate

Hate is one of many emotions,
Anger always at its strongest,
Danger all around you with no way to escape,
Red is a sign of danger, anger and blood.

Anger is like an erupting volcano,
A blast of hatred, fierce and angry,
Anger so serious you want to hurt someone,
Hate can cause a bitter-tasting revenge.

Hate is an emotion not to be toyed with.

Reece Wallace (11)
Archbishop Sumner CE Primary School

Love

Love is so shiny and white,
As white as the clouds in the sky,
Love can be a funny emotion,
It makes people smile.

Love is so benevolent,
It looks so bright,
It makes you tickle,
It's never dark - but always light.

Love is so sweet,
It sounds so peaceful,
Love is as clear as glass
And as beautiful as the ocean.

Love tastes like sugar,
It sounds like wedding bells,
It's a symbol of a dove,
Showing care and kindness is love.

Olayimika Olayanju-Olagbegi (10)
Archbishop Sumner CE Primary School

Anger

Anger, a feeling you can't control,
Something you can't let go of,
A dark blurred object.

Anger, a blazing big ball of fire heading for you,
A bitter taste on the tip of your tongue,
An explosion of rage deep inside of you.

Anger, is a never-ending maze,
It turns you into a fire-breathing dragon,
It takes over your soul.

Anger is more than a thought,
It's a sight . . .
And it's more than a sight . . .
It's a feeling.

Jordan Patrick-Asuman (11)
Archbishop Sumner CE Primary School

Who Am I?

I am as tall as a door,
I eat a lot of leaves,
I have long legs,
When I want to drink,
I stretch my legs, outwards and bend,
My legs are bent,
Look at me, what do you see?

Morayo Fadiya (8)
Archbishop Sumner CE Primary School

Who Am I?

Look at my fur as golden as coins,
Touch my tickly tail,
Taste my ranting roar,
Roar, roar,
I run madly,
I bite badly,
I am as dangerous as fire,
I roar in my wildcat's choir,
Who am I?

Ayeshia Adenugba (9)
Archbishop Sumner CE Primary School

Who Am I?

I am as fast as a speeding racecar,
I creep along the waving grass,
I am mysterious as a bumblebee,
Glowing in the dark,
I can run at full speed, *run, run, run,*
Miaow!
Miaow!
Miaow!
Miaow! Roar!
Look at my sensitive spotty skin,
Feel my soft fur,
Hear my miaows and roars in the
Middle of the night,
When you hear my miaows and roars,
Suddenly it will give you a fright,
Who am I?

Yohanna Ephrem (8)
Archbishop Sumner CE Primary School

Who Am I?

I'm as springy as can be
When I jump, I can touch
The tree.
Boing!
Bounce!
Croak!
Creak!
When I jump I can fly
Who am I?
When I come boinging by
You'll only see me in the sky!
Then I go into the water
To check up on my tadpole daughter,
I've journeyed back from the sky,
But can you tell me, who am I?

Daisy Chamberlain (8)
Archbishop Sumner CE Primary School

Who Am I?

Look at my meaty teeth,
Feel my twisty tail,
Touch my fluffy fur,
Hear my roar,
Taste my meat,
I sneak like a snake,
I run like the river,
Meat, meat for me,
I am as funny as a monkey,
With stripy soft skin.

Who am I?

Ryan Lawal (8)
Archbishop Sumner CE Primary School

Who Am I?

As smart as I am,
As sly as a snake,
Smart as a spider,
I am as wiggly as a wave,
As fierce as a fire,
What am I?
I wait for my prey to go
Over my head,
I snap and it
Is all dead.
What am I?

Matthew Lewis (8)
Archbishop Sumner CE Primary School

Who Am I?

I am as fast as can be,
Look at me,
I am king of the jungle possibly,
I am not scared, not sloppy,
Just eat anybody,
Roar, roar!
But sometimes I am lovely.

Guess who?

Guess who
Am I?

I have mates with cubs, got family too,
Guess, guess,
Who am I?

I hope you do.

Lauren Moseley (8)
Archbishop Sumner CE Primary School

Love

L ove is a red rose in the summertime,
O ver the rainbow, up into the clouds,
V aluable colours in the sky,
E very colour, bright and dull, which brightens you and I.

L ove is like a huge pink flower in the sky,
O ver the moon, stars and sun, far, high away,
V ery cuddly and comforting is the cloud where love lay,
E xcitement and joy is what love shows me.

Love is sweet like candyfloss and can be beautiful and sparkling,
Over the edges is where loves flies me.
Passion is the clouds, that's where love guides me,
Very soft is my heart.
Love is so kind,
I know we'll never part.
Enjoyable and sincere is how I feel with love around me,
Spicy and glittery is my heart to me.

Siana Douglas Keise (11)
Archbishop Sumner CE Primary School

Love

Love is sweet, it doesn't make you sad,
Love is special, it won't make you mad.
      You can't taste it,
      But you can feel it.
      You can't be it,
      But you can see it.

Love is gentle, it reminds you of the good times,
Including the good things that happened in your life.
      100% of love, that's what you'll get,
      Some things in your life that you'll never forget.

Love is calm, gentle and sweet,
Love is something that you will like to eat.
Love isn't bitter - love is nice,
Love is like eating chicken and lots of rice.

Isaac Danso (11)
Archbishop Sumner CE Primary School

Who Am I?

Mouth is as wide as a crocodile's
I like jumping in the Nile.

Splish
Splash
Splosh
Plop
I wiggle my tail like a crazy mad dog
I giggle and wiggle
My sounds are like a shriek
Never anything too bleak
Friendly, faithful
Always grateful.

Who am I?

Gabrielle Danso (8)
Archbishop Sumner CE Primary School

Guess Who?

I have two wings and a slim body,
I have two legs,
I have no beak,
I have antennae,
I am as colourful as a rainbow,
Who am I?

Abigail Sarpong (8)
Archbishop Sumner CE Primary School

My Evacuation

As I tumbled out of my cosy bed,
I was suddenly filled with a feeling of dread,
For today was the day of my evacuation
And I did not know what was my destination.

When I went downstairs to eat,
My mum and dad I did meet,
After breakfast they took out a sack
And told me that I should start to pack.

I packed my belongings - little had I,
A photo of my parents made tears prick my eyes,
With my case in my hand I was ready to go,
My family and I were full of woe.

As soon as I arrived at Barnes Station,
With no idea of what might be my location,
Some children were excited, some were sad,
I know what I felt, I felt bad!

I said my last goodbye to my ma
And I wished I didn't have to go so far,
Mum said, 'Go on, the train's about to go,'
But as I stepped inside I felt very low.

As the train rushed through the countryside,
I felt so sad and alone that I cried,
After I had dried my cheeks,
It felt as if I had been on the train for weeks.

Finally the train slowed down,
The place that we stopped at made me frown
And as we went into the town hall,
I saw a nice-looking lady with a shawl.

Some adults told us to stand in a line
And that everything would be fine,
Then other adults came to pick us
And I did wish that they wouldn't make such a fuss.

Soon I was chosen by the lady with the shawl,
I also noticed that she was very tall,
Then she showed me where she stayed
And I was so happy I could have hip hip hoorayed.

And now here I am, it's 2007,
Writing this poem about when I was eleven,
Even though it was all those years ago,
I will never forget those times of happiness and woe.

Madeleine Oliver (9)
Our Lady of Victories Primary School

My Evacuation

I cuddled my old, brown scruffy ted,
My parents and I were filled with dread,
I packed my belongings - few I had,
One was a picture of Mum and Dad.

My case in my hand, sad tears I shed,
I was leaving my home and my cosy bed,
The journey to the station - I hated it so,
The world around me was full of woe.

Barnes Station was busy, loads of people were there,
I was sad and worried but fully aware,
I said my last goodbyes, the whistle blew,
I stepped inside the train and away the train flew.

A carrier bag with food in the children had,
Biscuits and a chocolate bar, oh I was so glad,
I met some new friends and we ate together,
In the outside world there was terrible weather.

There were weird creatures outside on the green,
They were white with black dots and they looked very clean,
'Look, there are some cows!' my friends explained,
Is that what the creatures were actually named?

The train stopped and we arrived at a hall,
With my face so dirty, I looked like a fool!
We waited and waited until someone picked us,
The teachers told us we mustn't make a fuss.

At last a man picked me - from the army I thought,
He was holding a bag, that is all he brought,
I shyly followed the man, to his cart we walked,
He started to speak but in the end we *both* talked.

His house was white, it was very small,
I stepped inside its long, dark hall,
The kitchen was lovely - the floor was stone,
The bathroom was cold but I didn't start to moan.

My bedroom was dear, I had my own bed!
I unpacked my belongings and then I was fed,
The man was so kind, I loved him so,
He was like my father - I had forgotten my real one though.

I am so old now I can hardly remember,
The dreaded day at the beginning of September,
All day I sit in my comfy brown chair
And dream of the days when war was in the air.

Clemmie Pollard (9)
Our Lady of Victories Primary School

The War Of The Roses

There were once two families, who were always at war,
But soon it became a bit of a bore,
A lot of warriors carried a knife,
A lot of warriors were risking their life.

When Henry battled Richard in Bosworth Field,
Many warriors were easily killed,
So many people were on Richard's side,
Too many wives went in to hide.

The War of the Roses lasted 30 years,
The air was full of flying spears,
Richard was the White Rose, Henry was the Red Rose,
Richard's army was Henry's worst foes.

Many warriors were in fear,
One or two shed a tear,
When old Henry killed the king,
Many Lancastrians were about to sing.

Elizabeth of York was Henry's wife,
After that both families had a better life,
Henry VIII became a good knight,
He was someone no one in England wanted to fight.

Harry Bound (9)
Our Lady of Victories Primary School

My Evacuation

I remember the day of my evacuation,
I had to wake up to go to the station,
I took out my case and started to pack,
I got my gas mask which was black.

My mum was feeling very bad
And my dad was feeling very sad,
As I was walking down the lane,
I saw a Spitfire plane.

At the station, I waved goodbye,
I even saw children cry,
I got a big Cadbury's chocolate bar,
We had to go very far.

We soon arrived in a new place,
I hoped my host had a kind face,
We all lined up against the wall
And I saw a man that was cool.

He looked at me and said, 'Hello lad!'
But I was feeling very bad,
I looked up and said 'Hello!'
He seemed like a nice fellow.

We beat Hitler, the man,
At the end of the war, England and France had won,
In the countryside, I had loads of fun.

William Eacott (9)
Our Lady of Victories Primary School

My Evacuation

I remember the first day of my evacuation,
My mum told me to wake up early, but no explanation,
Then she said to me, there was a war,
Then I gave a great sigh of sadness and bore.

My mother and I got out my rucksack
And we started to pack a small snack,
Then Ma gave me a car toy,
But all I remember is jumping for joy.

Now I surely had some fears,
Slowly I began to shed some tears,
When we got to the very busy station,
I asked 'Where is our destination?'

I can't remember what she said,
So soon after I fled,
Next thing I knew I was on the train,
Waving goodbye again and again.

As my teacher quickly walked past,
I asked 'Has time gone past quite fast?'
She replied, 'Err I think so,'
Then I was filled with woe.

When we got to the big hall,
We were told to stand by the wall,
I was picked the very first,
But I was picked by the very worst.

For the house was very small,
I can't remember it all,
But I had horrid years,
Every night I would shed some tears.

Here I am in 2007,
Writing this poem about the sadness I saw,
I am glad I am back where I belong,
Singing my poem as I go along.

Lauren Wright (8)
Our Lady of Victories Primary School

My Evacuation

I remember the day of my evacuation,
I had to get up early to go to the station,
Before I went I had to pack,
In my bag I took a tasty snack.

Then we went to the station,
But my mum wouldn't give me an explanation,
I said my goodbyes and got on the train,
As the whistle blew I wondered if I would see,
My mum and dad again.

I got to the window and waved goodbye,
Then I gave a gigantic sigh,
Next I got down my heavy sack
And I took out my delicious snack.

Then the train came to a sudden stop at the town hall,
Next I had to line up against a cold wall,
One hundred children the crowd had to pick,
When you get someone you had to sign a certificate.

A man walked up to me and said, 'I'll be your host,'
We got to his house, it was enormous and very near the coast,
We were certainly not poor
And Germany will remember that we beat them
In the Second World War.

Conor Larkin (8)
Our Lady of Victories Primary School

Henry The VII And Richard III

Henry and Richard were going to war,
These two families had battles before,
The names of the families were Lancaster and York,
They both kept on fighting with spears and forks.

In the battle Richard fell down,
Henry killed him and he got the crown,
Henry was happy that he was now king,
He jumped for joy as he heard the birds sing.

But the Yorkists weren't happy as their king was dead,
They did not like Henry being the new head,
All the Yorkists cried and cried,
They had loved their good king but now he had died.

So Henry married Elizabeth, a Yorkist, in fact,
Now everyone was happy and that was that,
They had now joined the white rose and the red,
'Now that is a happy ending,' the people have always said.

Anthony Corless (8)
Our Lady of Victories Primary School

My Evacuation

I walked to the door, out of my bed,
I went downstairs and tears I shed,
I had to pack my bags for evacuation,
My mum wouldn't give me any explanation.

By now we were walking to the train,
I was crying hard but I could not complain,
Then I remembered the choc bar we all had,
We were not allowed to eat it, which made me sad.

Now we were waving to our mum and dad,
I cried and cried, I could not be glad,
I wanted to run home, but I was so sad,
The train started moving, I felt very bad.

After a long train ride, we got there at last,
A great big sigh, we got there not fast,
I looked at the tall people, they looked so cruel,
There was even one lady with a very big shawl.

One lady had seen me, she took me home,
In her front garden, there was a tall gnome,
Now I am writing in this very year,
But so many people were killed, oh dear.

Emily McMahon (8)
Our Lady of Victories Primary School

Henry VIII

There was once a battle at Bosworth field
And lots of people were being killed,
Even though they had their shields,
Richard lay dying on the hill.

Henry VIII became the new king,
He asked Elizabeth to wear his ring,
They came together as Lancaster and York,
Let's pop a lot of champagne corks.

Lancaster and York joined their roses as one,
Red was the bad rose and white was like the sun,
Red and white became the Tudor Rose.

Henry VIII was now the new head,
The Tudor Rose was white and red.

Jack Smith (8)
Our Lady of Victories Primary School

My Evacuation

I remember the day of my evacuation,
My mum would give me no explanation,
So I went with my mum to the station,
Immediately it started to rain.

From my eyes fell many tears,
I could be going away for years,
I was feeling very sad,
I would miss my mum and dad.

On the train I had a snack,
I looked in my bag to see what my mum packed,
When we arrived we went to a hall,
The children there were really small.

I was the last one there,
I didn't think that this was fair,
Then luckily for me I was picked,
By a woman with a stick.

At her home a good time I had,
But when the war ended, I was sad,
I liked it there, she bought me a bear,
When I look at it, I remember her care.

Andrew Porter (8)
Our Lady of Victories Primary School

My Evacuation

I remember the day of my evacuation,
I was to be taken to the station,
Before that, I was to pack,
My clothes, jacket and then a snack.

A cart arrived to take me there,
I waved goodbye and felt lonely and bare,
I did not want to leave my ma and pa
And I still did not know if I was so far.

Suddenly I arrived at a big crowded station,
Now I really wanted some explanation,
There were people young and old,
Some were hairy, and some were bald.

There I stood, sad and shy,
In my mind, I knew I shouldn't cry,
I suddenly heard some wheels coming near,
'Look,' I said, 'the train is here.'

I ran very quickly to the train,
I fell over, but I got up again,
There I stood, about to go on,
A lady stood there, she was waiting for something.

Ah ha, I thought, and I looked in my sack
And I handed her my ticket (which was black)
She smiled at me and let me in,
There were loads of children, fat and thin.

A minute later, the whistle blew,
I sat down and looked at the view,
Suddenly my sad memories came,
My ma and pa, would I see them again?

I wondered if my house would last?
Or if it would be bombed and blast?
Some children were crying very loud in pain
And some were ill and wanted to get off the train!

I was very tired and fell asleep,
A few hours later, I heard a peep,
We were there at long last,
I hoped I would have a blast.

A lady brought me to a hall,
She told me to stand by the wall,
Suddenly a lady came to me,
'Phew,' I said, I was very lucky.

The lady brought me to her lovely house,
She opened her front door which was as grey as a mouse!
I peeped inside before I went in,
The house was very clean (even the dustbin!)

I had a lovely time at the house of my host,
Some nights for dinner we would have roast,
One sunny morning my host said,
'Quickly hurry, get out of bed!'

She got me dressed as quick as she could
And took me to the neighbourhood,
There stood a very big train,
I was to be taken back to my lane.

I waved goodbye to my beloved host,
Whom I loved nearly the most!
So many tears she shed
And she waved once more and then fled!

Now I am sitting on my bedroom floor,
Writing this poem about the Second World War!

Jessica Taylor (8)
Our Lady of Victories Primary School

The War Of The Roses

There were once two families who were always at war,
From killing Richard's army Henry's arm was soon sore,
The War of the Roses had lasted thirty yeas,
Richard III's army were running out of spears.

Richard III's army were really getting very mad,
Because Henry VIII's army was getting very bad,
Henry VIII had waited a very long thirsty years,
But Richard III's army had shed very little tears.

Henry III was really getting very cross,
Because Richard III thought that he could be boss,
Henry pulled out his sword and hit Richard in the head,
Henry was alive and Richard was dead.

Henry VIII was now England's king
And together the white and red rose he would bring.

Lucas Tishler (8)
Our Lady of Victories Primary School

My Evacuation

I remember the day of my evacuation,
Today I was going to the station,
I was feeling excited and quite sad
And I knew the German's were very bad.

At the station I waved goodbye
And I tried very hard not to cry,
My parents did not know my location,
What would be my new destination?

On the train, I ate a chocolate bar,
But I was going ever so far,
After I had my chocolate bar, I felt a bit sick,
We arrived at the town, who would they pick?

A man came up to me, 'I'll have you,' he said,
At his house I had a huge bed,
I stayed with him till the end of the war,
Then at last my mum and dad I saw.

Declan Thompson (8)
Our Lady of Victories Primary School

Snow Falling

S now is falling everywhere,
N ever does in
O pen air,
W ow, look at that,
M an making a snowman,
A t the river loads of snow,
N ever seen this much snow before.

Daniel Bonner Hillier (10)
St John's CE Primary School, Penge

Winter Wonderland

Crunch, crunch, goes the snow under my feet,
I love this day, it's going to be a magnificent treat,
You may think it's fun, well it is a bit,
But sometimes it's not that much fun, cars are crashing
And people are slipping, but when it is fresh, it's nice,
It's a winter wonderland.

Amy Louise Brenson (9)
St John's CE Primary School, Penge

Snow Is Falling

Snow is falling, down and down,
I want to go out and play, now!
I want to go out and play because,
It doesn't snow every day,
Crispy, crunch and fresh,
Snow is falling,
I want to go out and play.

I dress up warm, all snug as a bug,
Thick layers are on my skin,
My clothes are squeezing in,
I put on my hat, my scarf and gloves,
Cool look, I saw a dove,
I want to go out and play now!

Can I go out and play for a tick?
Yes but be careful, the snow is thick,
I go out and play,
Just for a tick,
Mum is right,
The snow is thick!

Amy McLauchlan (9)
St John's CE Primary School, Penge

How I Love Snow

Watch the snow glow,
At night it's wonderful, it looks so bright,
You feel it, it's wet and damp,
Cold as the midnight breeze,
Falling down on those trees.

I prefer it cold like this,
'Teatime,' Mum shouts,
I throw a paddy and scream the outside down,
Going inside, it really upsets me,
On a night like this I feel so happy,
Just to be a part of the snow fights,
'Can I go out for one minute?'
'Right only for ten minutes.'

Uhh the snow starting to melt,
No more snow just freezing,
Cold ice on this wonderful night.

Rebecca Blizzard (9)
St John's CE Primary School, Penge

Snowballs

The snow is nice but . . .
If you do not have a warm coat,
It can be horribly cold.

If snowballs go in your ears,
It can be very disturbing.

Try and dodge snowballs
As best you can.

Try and find cover,
Then poke out and throw away!

Max Billy Edwards-May (10)
St John's CE Primary School, Penge

A Snowy Day

Snow is freezing,
Snow is cold,
Like ice on my road,
Crunchy ice falling down in my street
And in the town,
Snow is going everywhere,
Looking for a street that is bare,
Children having fun in the snow,
On the ground,
Deep below snow is going in the street,
Going below your feet,
Snow is like clouds in the sky,
Look everywhere it's so high!

Taja Hippolyte-Wells (9)
St John's CE Primary School, Penge

Beach

I stretch out my legs,
Digging my toes into the gooey sand.
I let the waves trickle over my feet,
I can feel the round shells knocking on my legs,
My warm back is cooled by the gentle breeze from the sea.
I skip over to the towering cliffs ahead of me.
I lick my chocolate ice cream,
Feeling the burst of iciness flowing down my throat,
As the last drop dissolves into a puddle on the sand,
I run to have a swim instead,
Then I lie back, floating on the sea,
Luxuriating in the sensation.
When the rosy sun sets I have to leave,
I wave to the sand, dusty, deserted and alone.

Jadzia Samuel (9)
St John's CE Primary School, Penge

Crunchy And Pure

It's crunchy and pure from way up high,
While coming from the sky!

It snows and snows with lovely delight,
It snows and snows, it's really bright!

Snow speeds to the ground
And you hear a pound!

You hear a silent noise
And you see a snowball fight with girls and boys!

Elliott Dyer (10)
St John's CE Primary School, Penge

Snowy Season

Now's the time to play in the snow,
The wind is still, going to blow,
But the children at the school don't mind,
They just want to crush and grind,
There are no leaves, left on the trees,
Just a chilly winter's breeze,
The children run about and play,
Until the snow, all melts away,
Then the children cried and wept in gloom,
But they knew the snow would be back soon.

Sadie Angela Jordan (9)
St John's CE Primary School, Penge

Snow

Do you see the snow gently falling?
A big white blanket that covers everything.

Falling so gracefully,
Dripping off the big tree.

Look a big snowman,
Footprints where we ran.

Snow looks like it's just been washed,
But our feet turn it to slush.

Siobhan McShane (9)
St John's CE Primary School, Penge

The Snow Angel

The snowman is cold,
The snowflakes glitter,
The angel is like ice,
The snow is very crunchy and pretty,
You can go on the sledge outside,
You can do snow angels
And you can throw snowballs at people.

Tia Jane Angel (10)
St John's CE Primary School, Penge

Poem On Greeks

Greeks, Greeks, wonderful Greeks,
What do you want to know about them,
They're smart, they're kind and good,
They do pottery and sing:
'All of us Athenians, ne, ne, ne,
We have all the good Gods and we
Have a great big key.'

Matthew Steenson (8)
St John's CE Primary School, Penge

School

My shoes are lace up,
My trousers and socks are grey,
My school shirt is white and
My tie is black and white,
In my school, that is the rule,
To wear this uniform,
My teachers are grand,
The children are fine,
That is why I am so divine.

Kyle Manning (9)
St John's CE Primary School, Penge

White Beautiful Snow

White, beautiful, crunching on my feet,
Very, very cold, it's like a treat.
Rolling a snowman up and down the ground
And if you listen closely it makes a crunchy sound.
Tomorrow I can't wait till it snows again,
Then I can play with all my great friends.

Emma Prempeh (10)
St John's CE Primary School, Penge

Snow

It makes me feel cold and excited,
It reminds me of playing a snowball fight,
It tastes like fresh water,
It smells like white fresh cloth,
It looks like a big ball when you're making a snowball,
Its colour is white and fresh and sweet.

Micheal Iluyomade (7)
Stockwell Primary School

Love

Love makes me feel happy and calm,
It makes me feel like someone taking care of me,
Love reminds me of when my mum hugs me, saying I love you,
Love tastes like . . . well really,
Love is a feeling that you can't taste,
Love smells like a flower that's just grown,
Love looks like someone who wants to take care of you
And I love that!

Zeinab Troare (8)
Stockwell Primary School

Mud

Mud makes me feel like making a mud cake
And it makes me feel happy,
I feel so excited when I see it,
Mud reminds me of chocolate custard in a pool
And it reminds me of a sticky chocolate river,
Mud tastes like chocolate caramel swirls,
Mud smells like melted chocolate éclairs,
Mud looks like a big brown sea made out of mud,
Mud is a sort of blacky brown colour.

Leila Bewshear (7)
Stockwell Primary School

Mud

Mud is horrible and icky,
Mud is slimy and soft,
When you pick mud up,
You feel like you have been overtook by mud aliens,
Mud tastes like horrible chocolate,
When I look at mud, it makes me feel ugly.

Scott Greenfield (8)
Stockwell Primary School

Rain

Rain makes me feel cold and happy,
It reminds me of a drink which tastes like water,
It smells like a big blue sea,
It looks like water and snow,
The colour is light blue.

Abdulhafiz Malak (7)
Stockwell Primary School

Can You Solve My Mystery?

Can you solve my mystery,
Which is dark and cold?
Can you solve my mystery,
That was never told?
Can you solve my mystery,
That shines like gold?
Can you solve my mystery,
Which is big and bold?
Can you solve my mystery,
That can never be sold?
Can you solve my mystery?

Aisha Lutumba (10)
Stockwell Primary School

Flowers

Flowers, flowers are so bright,
You can't get them out of sight,
Flowers, flowers everywhere,
You can put them in your hair,
Flowers, flowers are so pretty,
Some can even make you itchy,
Flowers, flowers are different colours,
Flowers, flowers, everyone likes flowers!

Salomé Ferreira Castro Silva (10)
Stockwell Primary School

Extreme Danger

Danger, danger waited for me,
Danger, danger I could not see,
It was here, it was there,
But did anyone care?
In my opinion danger is bad,
So look out for danger,
Yes you little lad.

Royan Moore (11)
Stockwell Primary School

Joy

Joyful is what I am,
Joyful is what made me,
I always smile,
I am never angry,
Joy is what turns my cheeks pink,
Joy sometimes makes me cry,
But I will always have a smile on my face,
As I pass people by,
Joyful is my family,
Joyful is my heart,
Joyful fills my heart,
In every single part!

Benedicte Makamu (9)
Stockwell Primary School

Arsenal

Arsenal is the best team in the world,
Especially Theirry Henry
And Francesc Fabregas
And the rest of the great players,
Arsenal rule,
So don't come bothering me with Chelsea or Man U,
Because Arsenal,
Arsenal rule!

We have Thierry Henry,
Who can score for fun,
We have Francesc Fabregas,
Who is our creative passing wonder kid,
We have Kolo Toure,
Who is a rock in defence,
We have Tomas Rosicky,
Who can score from midfield,
We have Gilberto,
Who does his job well,
We have Emmanuel Adebayor,
With his long hair,
We have Robin Van Persie,
Who scores for fun too
And many more great players too!

Tesfa Atere (9)
Stockwell Primary School

The Moon

The moon is a football,
High up in the sky,
The moon is an ice cream,
Thrown right through the clouds.

The moon is a yoghurt pot,
Kicked through the darkness of night,
The moon is a paint can,
Through the sky and clouds.

The moon is a rubber,
Thrown into space,
The moon is a pair of trainers,
Kicked off through the sky.

The moon is a scrunched paper,
That we bat through space,
Well, the moon is just,
A white splodge on a paper.

Aminah Turay (10)
Stockwell Primary School

Thankfulness

Thankfulness
Is being nice, so you
Won't pay the price.
Gratitude is not being
Rude, so you'll be
In a good mood.

We've got peace in
The UK,
So you'll have a
Nice day,
I'm thankful for my parents,
Who I adore,
I'm grateful for the love,
That the holy God gives from
Above.

Nana Akua-Afriyie (11)
Stockwell Primary School

The Clouds

The clouds are staring at me,
The rain is battering me,
While the clouds carry me,
The rain is jealous for me,
The clouds cry for me,
While the rain takes me away.

Tameka Salmon (11)
Stockwell Primary School

My Imagination

My name is Ellis but I'm not what I seem,
Dragons and pixies are all in my dreams,
My imagination is like no other,
I can imagine wizards and fairies with evil brothers.

Knights and witches, birds and bees,
Say anything and it would've been imagined by me,
Cyclops and minotaurs, I'm too advanced for that,
Why me; yes I invented the Hippalippalat!

My name is Ellis, but I'm not what I seem,
Dragons and pixies are all in my dreams . . .

Ellis Thomas (11)
Stockwell Primary School

Brings

Love brings joy,
Joy brings happiness,
Happiness brings courage,
Courage brings faith,
Faith brings belief,
Belief brings trust,
Trust brings desire,
Desire brings love!

Chelsea Beckford Tunisa (11)
Stockwell Primary School

My Name Is Honey

My name is Honey,
I am so sweet,
Have me on toast,
I am a treat,
I am delicious and runny
And really, really funny,
I can melt in your heart,
I am like a honey tart,
I can float in your dream,
Have me with cream,
I can brainwash your head
And make you go to bed.

Honey Brion Thompson (10)
Stockwell Primary School

My Feelings

Sometimes I feel down
And lost with nothing to do,
My mum will try and cheer me up,
Though I am still sad,
But I won't let my mum feel bad,
I think about the future
And watch TV all about nature,
Then I feel happy,
Jumping around the house,
While my auntie is changing
My cousin's nappy,
Now I am happy
And don't feel down!

Djenne Payne-Pemberton (10)
Stockwell Primary School

Anger

Anger, you made me hit the wrong person,
Anger, you made me lose all of my friends,
Anger, led me to such an unknown destination,
Anger, you are the mood I never miss,
Anger, next time I'll know which mood to choose,
Anger, all you need to know is that it definitely
Won't be you!

Hassan Mugga (10)
Stockwell Primary School

Anger And Being Happy

Anger is getting left out,
Anger is being picked on,
Anger is when someone shouts,
Anger is getting sent to bed,
Anger is getting no sleep on Sunday,
Anger is not being able to play out,
Anger is when parents say no to a pet,
Being angry is like being on a volcano when it is going to erupt!

Being happy,
I am the rink you ice skate around,
I am the pool you swim breaststroke in,
I am the paper wrapped around your presents,
I am the teddy you cuddle in bed,
I am the competition you win first prize in,
I am your voice singing a song,
I am everything,
I am you.
Being happy is the best thing in the world.

Kevaun McKenzie (10)
Stockwell Primary School

Friendship

The secret is what makes a friendship?
If there was no friendship,
What would happen to this world?
Would we be able to go outside?
What do you think?
Friendship is a thing that is stronger,
Than the universe, is bigger than
Anything and it makes the world much better!
Don't you think?
I wish there were friendship between
Everyone on this enormous world,
So that there wouldn't be lots of
Enemies between people!
Friendship is all you need!

Joâo Diogo Fernandes Conceicâo (10)
Stockwell Primary School

I Am Running, Running, Running

I am running, running, running,
I am running up the stairs,
But I'm never, never, never, never
Getting anywhere.

I am running, running, running,
But I'm going nowhere fast,
Now I'm huffing and puffing,
As I'm out of breath at last.

I am standing, with a grumble and a frown,
For the escalator beat me and it's
Taking me back down.

Ramone St Louis (11)
Stockwell Primary School

My Bunny Rabbit

My rabbit, my rabbit,
My soft bunny rabbit,
White, brown and yellow spots around his eyes,
And bounce up and down like a ping-pong ball.

My soft bunny rabbit,
Eats fresh carrots every day,
Drinks water from his water bottle,
And sleeps in his cosy cage
In the corner of my bedroom.

Ramon Oluseye (8)
Stockwell Primary School

Love

Love is the colour pink,
Love is like flowers and butterflies in the sky,
Love is someone that cares about you,
Love can be like stars in the sky,
Love can be like a soft pillow and a warm blanket,
Love can be your heart that beats in a rhythm,
Love is inside you,
Love is forever.

Ishmael Lartey (8)
Stockwell Primary School

Rain

Rain makes me feel wet and it makes me feel damp,
Rain reminds me of when I take a shower
And reminds me of drinking water.
Rain tastes like drinks,
Rain smells like dew from the ground and smells like Earth,
Rain looks like a spitball and a shower,
The colour of the rain is mixed blue and grey.

Tavio Wright (8)
Stockwell Primary School

Snow

Snow, snow, where do you go?
Snow please tell me,
I want to know,
Please tell me.

Why is it you are cold?
Like ice so I am told,
You melt into water
And sometimes you falter.

What do you do?
How I wish you were blue!
You're always on the road,
With your heavy load.

Tell me where you go,
Will you tell me in a mo?
Do you have a fear
When you're not here?

Please tell me where you go,
I really want to know.

Ryan Stoker (10)
Stockwell Primary School

Love

Love is a thing you can't see
the love of your heart as pink as your lips
When I touch you I hear lips
You smell like perfume
and when you enter the room
you and me are only apart with beating heart.

I have one rose
that is as soft as your nose
Love feels like the touch of your face
with you I feel safe
Love sounds like the beautiful sky
and my head goes round and round
with my heart-beating sound
Love reminds me of happy times
with love I feel like a dove
as free as a dove.

Nicole Jessica Figueira de Sousa (7)
Stockwell Primary School

Cinderella's Dress

The kitchen mice sing as they run, run, run,
'We will spin the sparkle of the sun, sun, sun.
We will spy lots of treasures in the town, town, town,
We will find nine buttons for her gown, gown, gown.
We will take blue feathers for her bed, bed, bed,
We will ask the spiders for their thread, thread, thread.
We will catch the colours of the skies, skies, skies,
We will match the dazzle of her eyes, eyes, eyes.
We will steal the ripples of the seas, seas, seas,
We will add the rustle of the trees, trees, trees.
We will snip the flowers from the grass, grass, grass,
We will make two slippers out of glass, glass, glass.
We will sew the starlight of her hair, hair, hair,
We will weave a wonder that is rare, rare, rare.
And Cinderella shall be so rich, rich, rich,'
The kitchen mice sing as they stitch, stitch, stitch.

Anastasia Carvalho (7)
Stockwell Primary School

Why, Why, Why

Why, why, why can't I fly, fly, fly?
Why, why, why am I shy, shy, shy?
Why, why, why don't I feel alright?
Why, why, why can't I fight?
Why, why, why do I look so weak?
Why, why, why do I have a purple beak?
Why, why, why can't I let it show?
Why, why, why? I don't know.

Why, why, why are my hands turning blue?
Why, why, why? It's because of you.
You were my friend but now you're gone,
When you were here the light just shone.
But now I'm alone like a dog with no bone,
It's no use and it's not fair,
So many hours and years to share.
Why do I moan? It's no use, nowhere,
Some day I will see you up there in the sky,
But you went before me I don't know why.

Ana Gomes (10)
Stockwell Primary School

My Best Teacher - Miss Aitogi

M iss Aitogi is the best,
'I like chocolate,' she says all the time,
S he's a chocoholic lady,
S he's the best teacher in the world.

A lways funny, Faye Aitogi,
I like her, I like her, I like her,
T eachers drink too much coffee,
O n and on eating chocolate,
G et a grip of it, chocolate is the best!
I like her, I like her, I like her!

Payge Gregory (9)
Thorntree Primary School

Miss Carmen

Miss Carmen is funny,
On days that it is funny,
On days that it rains,
Miss Carmen has to use her brains,
On days that it is snowing,
Miss Carmen is glowing,
On every other day,
Miss Carmen is OK!

Luke Cheal (9)
Thorntree Primary School

Snake Poem

Slippery, slimy snake slides
Through the jungle,
Scares the other animals,
Eats creepy-crawlies,
Then its gazing eyes
Stare at its food,
Then the next second,
Ssss . . . the food is gone.

Esther Agbara (9)
Thorntree Primary School

Debby

D ebby is helpful,
E verybody likes her,
B uzzing in the classroom,
B uzzing in your ear,
Y ou are a fool if you go near her.

Tommy Amis (8)
Thorntree Primary School

My Dog

My dog is called Maisy,
But I call her Spaghetti Bolognese . . .
She's always eating food,
Whatever is her mood,
Then she has a long nap,
Sitting on my mum's lap.

George Ball (9)
Thorntree Primary School

Happiness

Happiness is going to Wolverhampton,
Happiness is going to the park,
Happiness is going to the beach,
Happiness is going to see my cousins,
Happiness is when it's the weekend,
Happiness when you smell chocolate,
Happiness is when you go to the cinema.

Sade Sangar (7)
Thorntree Primary School

Happiness

Happiness is like a jacuzzi,
Happiness feels like watching TV in bed,
Happiness feels like flying with my bike,
Happiness is going on holiday,
Happiness is going to the pub,
Happiness feels like a bag of chips.

Danny Fryer (7)
Thorntree Primary School

Happiness

Happiness sounds like the school gates
Closing on a Friday afternoon,
Happiness tastes like a nice juicy steak,
Happiness smells like strawberry cheesecake,
Happiness looks like watching TV,
Happiness feels like a warm day,
Happiness reminds me of going on a bike ride
And going swimming.

Quinn Smith-Suckoo (7)
Thorntree Primary School

Things I Will Do In Ten Years' Time

When I am old, I will go to the shops by myself,
Go to Spain,
Going to a movie,
Visit my mum and move out,
Get a job,
Get more friends,
Have a baby and if it is a girl,
I will call her Emma and if it is a boy,
He will be called Ben.

Darcy Clinton (7)
Thorntree Primary School

When I Grow Up

When I grow up,
I want to be a fantastic famous popstar,
I want to travel for miles and miles
In a shiny bright red car.

When I grow up,
I want to have a Rottweiler in my case,
One that does not bite or scratch,
One that's run in a race.

When I grow up,
I'll be the complete queen of me,
Then no one can tell me what to do,
Not even the King of Paris.

When I grow up,
I want to be a fantastic famous popstar,
I want to travel for miles and miles
In a shiny bright red car.

Katie Chapman (7)
Thorntree Primary School

Happiness

Happiness sounds like a river going by,
Happiness tastes like a big, juicy sandwich,
Happiness smells like a cone of chips,
Happiness looks like the biggest ice cream in the world,
Happiness feels like summer and being out of school,
Happiness reminds me of puppies.

Abbie Carter (8)
Thorntree Primary School

Happiness

Happiness feels like a good jacuzzi,
Happiness feels like a sponge,
Happiness tastes like a cake,
Happiness tastes like ice cream,
Happiness feels like a hot bubblebath,
Happiness feels like I'm happy,
Happiness looks like a giant fire,
Happiness looks like me,
Happiness smells like a hot dog,
Happiness smells like salty sea,
Happiness sounds like a storm,
Happiness sounds like the wind,
Happiness feels like my friends,
Taymarie and Celine.

Ibukun Agbara (7)
Thorntree Primary School

When I Grow Up

When I grow up, I'll be a popstar
And have a cool voice,
I'll be a nurse and have loads of money in my purse
And maybe a teacher too.

When I grow up, I'll be big and strong
And as tall as a tree
And I won't be scared of anything,
Even a buzzing bee.

When I grow up, I'll find a husband,
Have children and get married.

When I grow up, I'll live in Egypt,
Have my own holidays and go where I want
And do what I want.

When I grow up, I'll stay up late,
Clean the floors and polish the plates.

When I grow up, I'll cook whatever I want,
Without using a book.

When I grow up, I'll own a Ferrari,
I'll even have a horse in a barn and
Have hundreds of pets.

When I grow up, I won't go to school,
I'll buy a pool and - tools.

When I grow up, I'll be kind and helpful,
Be an author and eat only a quarter of fruit a day.

When I grow up, I'll chat like my mum.

When I grow up, I'll go out on my own
And have my own home.

When I grow up, I'll be as happy as can be.

Rebeccah Love (7)
Thorntree Primary School

Happiness

Happiness is chocolate and ice cream,
Happiness is looking at stars,
Happiness is sleeping,
Happiness is for life,
Happiness is dogs playing,
Happiness reminds me of having good fun,
Happiness is happiness,
Happiness is my family.

Joseph Newman (7)
Thorntree Primary School

Happiness

Happiness sounds like a bubbling jacuzzi,
Happiness tastes like a chocolate cake,
Happiness smells like a juicy hot dog,
Happiness looks like a sunny beach,
Happiness feels like a summer holiday,
Happiness reminds me of staying in bed.

Salma Salah (7)
Thorntree Primary School

Happiness

Happiness sounds like playing a good game,
Happiness tastes like chocolate cake,
Happiness smells like ice cream,
Happiness looks like you're smiling,
Happiness feels like a leather sofa,
Happiness reminds me of a jacuzzi.

Matthew Coleman (8)
Thorntree Primary School

Happiness

Happiness is like chocolate and custard,
Happiness is going to the park,
Happiness is like a cuddly teddy,
Happiness is like steamy toast,
Happiness is going to the beach,
Happiness is like sizzling sausages.

Sam Green (8)
Thorntree Primary School

When I Grow Up

When I grow up,
I will have a driver's license and
Drive anywhere in the world,
When I grow up,
My job will be a demolisher,
When I grow up,
I want to be rich,
I'd like to have £6,000 and
Live in a castle,
When I grow up,
I will drive a Beetle car.

George Power (7)
Thorntree Primary School

Happiness

Happiness is a chocolate cake,
Happiness is a chocolate Flake,
Happiness is smiles all around,
Happiness feels like a jacuzzi,
Happiness is me cuddling my teddy.

Harrison O'Donoghue (7)
Thorntree Primary School

As

As mad as Barney,
As cold as water,
As big as a lion,
As small as a rat,
As smelly as a dog,
As cuddly as a cat,
As bad as Kevin,
As funny as Tom,
As silly as James B,
As short as Jack D.

Kristen Tedham (10)
Thorntree Primary School

I Know Someone Who Can

I know someone that is so stubborn,
I know someone that lives in an oven,
I know someone that is so green,
I know someone that looks like a bean,
I know someone that can
Supercalifragilisticexpialidocious,
I know someone, who can do a handstand for seven hours,
I know someone that is a football,
I know someone that can be so cool,
I know someone that can act like a monkey,
I know someone that can ride a donkey
And that someone is *you!*

Connor Gregory (10)
Thorntree Primary School

I Saw

I saw the sun shining,
I saw a person dining,
I saw the Earth's core,
I saw a penny on the floor,
I saw a flying fish,
I saw sausage on a dish,
I saw Mr Driver,
I saw a fiver,
I saw a house on fire,
I saw a car's tyre,
I saw the blue sky,
I saw a person die,
I saw a white board,
I saw a real sword.

Glenn Nutton (10)
Thorntree Primary School

My Word Party

Loving words clutch your heart,
Rude words make burps and sparks,
Sly words catch and sneak,
Short words come nice and sleek,
Common words are hard on your head,
Swear words are very rare,
Hard words are really bare,
Foreign words get in a huddle,
Careless words get in a muddle,
Long words are very tiring,
Code words are always firing,
Silly words I like to use,
Hyphenated words often confuse,
Strong words are *big* and *bold,*
Sweet words you can hug and hold,
Small words help our tongues,
Till at last the morning comes,
Kind words give out Roses . . .
Snap! The dictionary closes.

Georgie Devito (10)
Thorntree Primary School

The Word Concert

Loving words clutch like two people in a hutch,
Rude words are not very nice and we hate so much,
Sly words sneaking like a fox,
Short words can fit in a box,
Common words we all know,
Complicated words make us really low,
Swear words are terribly rude,
Hard words change your mood,
Foreign words run down a stream,
Careless words are very mean,
Long words reach from here to Venice,
Code words are such a menace,
Silly words are what you say when you drink wine,
Hyphenated words have a line,
Strong words are muscly,
Sweet words are cuddly,
Small words are like little hums,
Kind words give out Roses . . .
Snap! The dictionary closes.

Kiera Murphy (10)
Thorntree Primary School

Similes

As smart as a teacher,
As cold as ice cream,
As fluffy as my teddy,
As sly as a fox,
As slimy as a snail,
As fast as a cheetah,
As clear as water,
As big as a boulder,
As smooth as ice,
As sticky as glue,
As tall as a giraffe,
As colourful as a rainbow,
As green as grass,
As blue as the sea,
As yellow as cheese,
As red as blood,
As brown as chocolate,
As bright as a light,
As hard as a brick,
As hot as pepper,
As happy as a puppy,
As white as teeth,
As shiny as glitter,
As dry as the desert,
As gold as a wedding ring,
As cheeky as a monkey,
As bleak as the winter,
As thin as paper,
As thick as a book,
As good as I get.

Danielle White (10)
Thorntree Primary School

The Word Disco

Loving words clutch like a chain,
Rude words are dumb and a pain,
Sly words can take the heat,
Short words are lovely and sweet,
Common words are up to our heads,
Complicated words you feel like ripping to shreds,
Swear words get you into trouble,
Hard words you should learn on the double,
Foreign words never get in,
Careless words are pointless things,
Long words go for miles,
Code words are worthwhile,
Silly words should be shipped up the Nile,
Hyphenated words give me grime,
Strong words stick to the page,
Sweet words can be my slave,
Small words are not careless,
Till the last morning comes,
Kind words give out happiness,
Snap! The dictionary closes.

Ryan Carter (10)
Thorntree Primary School

I Saw

I saw a cat with green hair,
I saw my mother dancing with a bear.

I saw some beetles getting big and huge,
I saw a cat saying, 'You are going to lose.'

I saw a hand without any fingers,
I saw a choir without the singers.

I saw my friend with a hand of fire,
I saw a girl with a foot made of wire.

I saw a rainbow as black as night,
I saw a wire without a light.

I saw a wizard with a lady's hat,
I saw a mouse eating a bat.

I saw a fish attacking a shark,
I saw a lion eating bark.

I saw some ants going *thump* on the ground,
I saw an elephant not making a sound.

Stephanie Rouse (10)
Thorntree Primary School

The Months Of The Year

January brings a heavy breeze
And also brings a tiny freeze.

February is sweet but also sour
And also has its first blue flower.

March is the month that brings newborn
And a yellow plant that is called corn.

April has rainy showers,
Passes by like a million hours.

May is like gorgeous hot buns
And also hot as the burning hot sun.

June is red as all those roses,
Children dance and do some poses.

Scorching July,
Is a fat lie.

August brings those nice brown leaves
And don't forget those scary keys.

September oh no, here comes frost,
Just make sure you don't get lost.

October is that scary month,
You better watch out for those monster munch.

November is that tricky month,
Make sure you don't galumph.

December is freezing cold,
Look in your sandwich, there might be mould.

Asten Brown (10)
Thorntree Primary School

Simile Poem

As soft as a dog,
As hard as a log,
As long as a snake,
As small as a milkshake,
As loud as a bellow,
As quiet as a cello,
As slow as a snail,
As fast as a gale,
As clear as glass,
As green as grass,
As grey as the sky,
As bad as a lie,
As nice as sweets,
As bad as feet,
As thin as a ruler,
As thick as a Mini Cooper,
As big as brass,
As tiny as the class,
As interesting as a book,
As good as a cook,
As pretty as a lady,
As smart as a baby,
As cold as a lake,
As fat as a cake,
As smelly as tuna,
As terrible as Mr Driver's Laguna.

Storm Smith-Suckoo (10)
Thorntree Primary School

As . . .

As soft as a wall,
As fast as a snail,
As hot as ice,
As straight as a worm,
As big as an ant,
As heavy as a pencil,
As cold as the sun,
As juicy as water,
As long as a pie,
As small as a nit,
As nice as crocodiles,
As silly as a bird,
As short as a snake,
As crazy as a bat,
As hairy as a spider,
As hard as a ruler.

Marie-Jo Djedje (11)
Thorntree Primary School

All The Colours In The World

Darkness is the colour of black,
It's like walking through a dark house and finding a cat.

Funny is the colour of yellow,
It's like the colour of the bright yellow sun.

Love is the colour of red,
It's like a sweet red rose.

Fear is the colour of blue,
It's like trying to breathe under the sea.

Marriage is the colour of pink,
It's like you're a whole new person.

Zoe Rennie (10)
Thorntree Primary School

I Like Colours

Love is the colour of cheeky pink,
Like beautiful, gleaming roses,
Swaying in the wind.

Fun is the colour of silver,
Like a sparkling diamond twinkling in the sun.

Darkness is the colour of black,
Like being locked in a cupboard,
No sound but scary and dark.

Laughter is the colour of purple,
Like true love in a park.

Zoë Mansbridge (9)
Thorntree Primary School

Rainbow Colour

Love is baby-pink because it is for a pink rose,
Fear is black like you are walking down the street,
Hate is dark black like dirty mud,
Happiness is gold like marmalade dripping off my spoon,
Sadness is grey like a funeral day,
Anger is dark green like grass.

Donique Shallow (9)
Thorntree Primary School

Rainbow

Darkness is jet-black, like a haunted house on a dark, dark night,
Happiness is the colour purple, it is like you're at a funfair,
Love is the colour red like red roses, soft and beautiful,
Fear is the colour brown like mud,
Sadness is the colour blue like the deep, cold ocean.

Zoë Mullord (9)
Thorntree Primary School

Colours

Funny is pea-green,
It is funny watching a pig rolling in a muddy puddle.

Marriage is white,
For a beautiful dress.

Nosy is brown,
It can be annoying sometimes.

Kindness is pink,
For no bullying, everyone can have fun.

Kayley O'Donoghue (9)
Thorntree Primary School

Colours!

Love is like a pink, beautiful, blooming rose
Shining in the bright sun.

Happiness is like lemon-yellow like some pretty flowers.

Darkness is like black, like a scary, spooky, haunted house.

Fun is like orange like a big, fat, juicy orange
That you can eat.

Sadness is like grey, like a really gloomy day.

Hate is like red, like a lot of danger ahead.

Chloe Burton (9)
Thorntree Primary School

Colours And Feelings!

Love is lilac like a patch of violets growing in a field,
Hate is a glittering silver, the colour of shattered glass
Stuck through a bleeding heart,
Cheekiness is orange like squeezing oranges into a broken juicer,
Darkness is black like Dracula's cape,
Draping on the path of the vampire's cemetery,
Silence is white like angels in Heaven,
Singing Christmas carols,
Hunger is grey, like a starving tramp dying in the cold,
Colours, colours, colours they show what we are feeling!

Lucy Newman (9)
Thorntree Primary School

I Like Colours

Love is the colour of pink,
It sounds like a ruby-red rose,
It tastes like raspberries handpicked from the garden,
It smells like beautiful flowers,
It looks like a rose.

Fun is the colour of golden yellow,
It sounds like a burning sun,
It tastes like a fresh lemon,
It smells like a summer's day,
It looks like a golden sun.

Claire Slaughter (10)
Thorntree Primary School

The Colours Of The Rainbow

Yellow is happy just like the sun,
Orange is sweet just like an orange,
Red is like love between two people,
Pink melts the love and stains it forever,
Violet is like laughter just like kids' jokes,
Blue is exciting like getting a puppy,
Green is like happiness like running in a meadow,
Brown burns like your mum's overdone cookies,
Black is like prison where criminals go,
So now you know the colours of the rainbow.

Kayleigh Grant (10)
Thorntree Primary School

Colours

Fear is the colour of red fire dragons,
Love is the colour red from a relationship,
Hate is pure *black* as dirty as mud,
Happiness is the colour of pure white paper,
Sadness is baby-blue like the sky.

Brandon Bissenden (10)
Thorntree Primary School

Colours

Love is the colour of a sweet pink flower
With a tender red centre,
This smells like a sweet pink guava.

Anger is the colour of rage fire,
This looks like a fire-breathing dragon,
Burning down your house.

Anger is the colour of orange,
It feels like a pain of burning fire
Rushing through my body.

Darkness is the colour of pitch-black,
This feels like a spooky bat
Swooping over a black cat.

Chinua Joseph-Collins (9)
Thorntree Primary School

Colours

A dark scary cave is jet-black,
A sunflower is as yellow as the shining bright sun,
A flower, indigo and eye-catching,
As blue as the deep blue sea,
As pink as a light rose,
As gold as a shining ring.

Scott Richard (10)
Thorntree Primary School

Jack's Perfect Poem

Red is the colour of fun,
Blue is the colour of laughter,
Yellow is the colour of people having a laugh,
Orange is the colour of hunger,
Indigo is the colour of my favourite film 'Ed, Edd and Eddy',
Violet is the colour of my mum's dress,
Baby-blue is the colour of the lovely beach sky,
Green is the colour of summer grass,
Brown is the colour of caramel chocolate,
Jet-black is the colour of the Charlton kit,
All of these colours came straight from my head,
Now I will give you some more,
Roar-red is the colour of the Arsenal kit.

Jack Lee Kiely (9)
Thorntree Primary School

My Colours

Fear is black like a dark cave with dark eyes shining in the darkness,
Love is pink like a shining pretty rose,
Hate is grey like the dark, stormy night sky,
Happiness is gold like the shining sun,
Sadness is blue like the deep blue sea,
Anger is red like losing a race,
Silence is silver like a spy,
Laughter is yellow like a sunflower that's in bloom,
Fun is peach like your best friend,
Hunger is brown like a juicy chicken,
Darkness is black like a creepy cave with glowing red eyes.

Jamie Seymour (9)
Thorntree Primary School

Colours With Meanings

Fear is black like seeing in the night,
Love is white-pink hearing angels sing in choirs,
Hate is like broken red and shattered right through your head,
Happiness is like light blue and floating on a candy cloud,
Sadness is a broken heart and crying tears of sorrow,
Anger is someone being killed then screeching tyres in my ears,
Silence is the sound of a harp playing peaceful music,
Laughter is purple like a tasty grapefruit,
Fun is gold like toy Heaven,
Hunger is like wanting food but hallucinating it,
Darkness is like Dracula's blood dripping from his fangs.

Chukwuma Aliago (9)
Thorntree Primary School

Colours!

Black is like a haunted house with silky
Cobwebs and shattered windows,
Sky-blue is like the beautiful deep blue sea,
Red is as red as any rose,
Peach is like a big juicy peach to eat,
White is as white as Michael Jackson's skin,
Brown is like a delicious bar of chocolate,
Shining yellow is like the magnificent sun,
Shining down on the sandy beach,
Mauve is like a beautiful felt-tip pen,
Smoky grey is like a smelly bin,
Lime green reminds me of horrendous stinky feet,
Pink is like love from one of Cupid's arrows,
Orange feels like you're relaxing in the bath,
Bronze, silver and gold make you feel like you've won an award,
An inky blue feels like it's time to say bye,
So goodbye!

Alex Coleman (10)
Thorntree Primary School

Charlie's Perfect Poem

Fun is all sorts of colours,
Playing with all our brothers,
Sometimes I just wish to lie in my covers.

Darkness is a jet-black,
I would never turn back,
Otherwise I'll get the sack.

Anger is ruby-red,
When you are frustrated,
It turns the colour of your head.

Jealousy is like the glistening, green grass,
Shattering like a window screen glass.

As gold as an Egyptian stone,
As old as a broken bone,
If the mummy comes after me,
I would run straight home!

Charlie Barrett (9)
Thorntree Primary School

The Titanic

The death of many people,
On a sinking ship,
Most of them were killed,
As it started to tip,
To America it went,
But it sunk very low,
As the people started screaming,
No! No! No!

All filled with water,
The Titanic sunk,
Everyone in their beds
And everyone in their bunks,
The lifeboats lowered,
The children cried,
The parents waved goodbye,
Before they all died.

Oliver Marlow (8)
Thorntree Primary School

West Ham United

W e all like West Ham United,
E specially me,
S ome people think we can do better,
T hey don't know what they are talking about!

H ow can they be at the bottom of the Premiership?
A lan Curbishley is the manager,
M aybe he will be West Ham's manager for years!

U pton Park is their home ground,
N ewcastle is their next match,
I support them every day,
T hey try their best in every game,
E ven when it is pouring with rain,
D own the Hammers go but still I love them!

Leighvi Pilcher (9)
Thorntree Primary School

What Do The Animals Think?

I am climbing through the jungle,
When I hear a human shout,
'Look at this gorilla,
We could catch it without a doubt!'
Why were they chasing me?
There was nothing I could do,
They put me straight to sleep
And I woke up in a *zoo!*
I was trapped inside a cage with *no* trees to climb,
At least other animals,
Could help pass the time.

Lots of people pass and go,
Staring closely at me,
Children stare in wonder as if there's much to see!
Later I was moved away by someone I knew,
To a big safari park, it's *much* better than the *zoo!*

Carl White (9)
Thorntree Primary School

Monday's Child

Monday's child is dark and sad,
Tuesday's child is happy and mad,
Wednesday's child is clever and bright,
Thursday's child is cute and light,
Friday's child is calm and gentle,
Saturday's child is wild and mental,
But if you're a Sunday's child you are
Healthy and wise and you can never lie.

Christina Summerfield (10)
Thorntree Primary School

Silliness

Some people are silly,
Some are not,
Some are very silly,
But I'm not!

When I was walking in the shops
I saw stupid people
I saw stupid people licking lollipops.

When I was walking down the shore,
Then I got knocked over by a huge boar.
Then I heard a huge wave it roared,
'So am I silly?'

Daisy Golding (8)
Thorntree Primary School

Young Writers Information

We hope you have enjoyed reading this book - and that you will continue to enjoy it in the coming years.

If you like reading and writing poetry drop us a line, or give us a call, and we'll send you a free information pack.

Alternatively if you would like to order further copies of this book or any of our other titles, then please give us a call or log onto our website at
www.youngwriters.co.uk

Young Writers Information
Remus House
Coltsfoot Drive
Peterborough
PE2 9JX
(01733) 890066